MELTWATER

MELTWATER

Craig Evenson

Clare Songbirds
Publishing House

Clare Songbirds Publishing House Poetry Series
ISBN 978-1-957221-25-0
Clare Songbirds Publishing House
Meltwater© 2025 Craig Evenson

Printed in the United States of America
FIRST EDITION

140 Cottage Street
Auburn, New York 13021
www.claresongbirdspub.com

for better
for worst
for margaret
always

All of these poems have previously appeared elsewhere. For permission to print, and for assignment copyrights to him, the author is grateful to the editors and publishers of the following:

Barrow Street, Blueline, The Café Review, Cardinal Sins, Chiron Review, Common Ground Review, Connecticut River Review, Evening Street Review, Free State Review, Futures Trading, The Hurricane Review, Illuminations, INSCAPE, Iodine Poetry Journal, Fractal, Indefinite Space, Lalitamba, Lost Coast Review, The Louisville Review, The Main Street Rag, The Mid-America Poetry Review, The Midwest Quarterly, Off the Coast, Out of Our, Paper Nautilus, Pilgrimage, Progenitor, The Radvocate, River Oak Review, River Poets Journal, Riding Light, Sheepshead Review, Sierra Nevada Review, Spectrum, Straylight, The Same, The Stillwater Review, Tiger's Eye, Torrid Literature Journal, West Trade Review, WINK, Your Impossible Voice.

Contents

Vernal

Math of tilt.
Tender angles
open, close,
fuse and smolder
toward split
into clear heart's energy,
a slow commotion
singing in villages
of delirious gods
who live inside two walls
and don't notice your dog
spilling a great flower-full of water
on the dirt floor.
They leave their houses and gardens
to addicts and maniacs,
would mulch you like a stump for your dullness
as easily as they part their wings,
beaten into the teeth of order
by echoes
in their hollow bones.

Playground Legend

Mad rain and the mud
ran from the thing of armor
drawing its crenellate tail up
the grayed green slope.
Crawling obscurity
terrestrial cloud
hovered in the valley of the shadow
of the monkey bars to nudge and swallow
a sodden duckling;
plodded uninvited into the deep grass
settled its pebbled legs
into the earth
of the brooding larks.

August

dropped songs
mulched in sharp shadows
changed angles
of crows' voices
farther off than their feathers

treetops paw
the sunned grass
the season of pause
the end of a suspended breath
before the steady inhalation of green

swallowtail, sunflower
monarch, oxeye, coneflower,
maple, oak, sumac, pause,
before the orderly forgetting of names

August

Since the world's not going to stop dying soon
there are bills, poems,
parents' albums and letters.
If not children, something else
will drag us into the dimming future.
The cicadas,
an animal that, after years in the ground,
unburies itself to die,
have begun their keening,
their corpses here and there
buried in light and air, defining
in their time above ground
the season of summer stopping
to look at what's been done again.
The robins remain unconcerned
and the crows rustle,
druids in the dark canopy
sometimes flying a short span
to another branch
as if to evade the cicadas' auroglyphs
cutting into heavy air
while a swallowtail,
brief life,
suns itself,
out-quieting death
on a maple leaf.

Grackles

Spring-sprung
                  sun-spun grackles grazing
shackled   intent
together   four
                    black blazes
    slangy neighborhood
                        gang swagger
strut   check   hop
                          strike
light
flit
                lit birds

From the Parking Lot

Sunrise.
The string of water
at the pasture's edge
came out of the darkness,
a fatted marsh
of melted snow.
It returns
with the unrippled interest
of a gracious host—
ecstatic barrel roll,
stretched extremities,
earth-echoed whispers of commotion
through the hollow bones
of the first goose
out of the sky.

Crow and Sky

Having bathed in the brook
the crow in the oak has selected for his folded
    elegance
a bare, golden limb with a view
on the field where he will nab
young rabbits, mice, nip the odd
    pheasant nest,
each flight
feather patiently taken
into the bill amid the trill of insects,
the whispered thrill of a warm breath
of sky, eye deep in feathers,
the smart zip, hook, and catch
of barbules up the shaft, eyes
averted, eyes shut maybe dreaming
of his own perfect blackness

until each barb of every feather
is ready as a wedding suit. Fresh,
wanting to be held, he turns
    his eyes out,
gives a lusty shout, and hurtles
to his beloved.

Doppler Incident

I read and feel whiter
page by orderly page,
nudge into days
without tendencies,
over smothered edges
of sudden juts
into the cup and shell
of the breath of earth,
rigid distance
bereft of dread

now unfettered
by a snap of the eyes:
snapped and slanted trunks of trees
piles of night and light heaped
one onto the other and back
white trunks and limbs tossed
into Chinese characters
needled and razored through
to liquid sky limit
of lily pads unscarred
by sparks thrown off the gray lake
before the grinding wind
speeding on feathered bits
breaking on strands of moments like igloos

Tonight the Snow is Not Falling

it's dropping
too sharp for thought
as if that were its unfortunate job:
slice to mist
every word
but the ones that can walk
on its edge,
the dangerous way everything happens,
each flake a straight trail
intersected a thousand quiet times
endowing the dark
intricate nights
of unleaved branches
saying each needle
each note of birdsong,
the ache of existence,
my frozen hands
on the shovel's handle.

Thaw

In the next room they're
talking about the world.
In back the bench
and branches are piled with fresh snow.
Even the twigs hold their share.
A nuthatch climbs, all intent,
around the conked trunk of an ash tree.
Spring is coming
as surely as the end of the world.
We feel its appetite from a thousand miles,
its songful breath veiling the tinnitus of winter.

The wet heavy snow
smiles even as it melts,
flows gleefully along the curb,
falling into the storm drain,
heading home with a howl.

Winter poems ,
laid out like birds
poorly preserved in darkness
and house-cracking order,
walk their legs upon the earth
remember
how it is coming
into the room
they've spent months
making for it,
relieved now
of everything
water is not.

Prayers

Sharp as glass,
a stone enclosing
a hammering heart,
Maze wants nothing but
to sink her teeth into the autumn
fat of this grazing groundhog,
face bowed in attendance,
lost in thoughtlessness
of silent incisors
a feast
of forgetting
to look up
forgetting
that almost every day
of this exquisite August pause
we've sent him trundling for the raspberry patch
       until a wind imprints the creek
twinkling the cottonwood leaves
fills with our scent
and he freezes
looks usward for a held breath
remembers!
shatters himself and the dog
into a run for the thicket.

Easter Storm

All day the wind wore white.

If birds had beliefs they wouldn't

Believe their eyes and ears,
their steady streams of meaning.

They'd spend days thinking twice about who.
They'd sharpen their beaks, gather thorns,

find their rest in a wing and a prayer,
the restless uninfected moving

through weather and loss
on quick wings and a song.

Wolf Flow

Stops for a whisper
body swap
paws on spruce toes,
then up against
the frenzied gravity
of blackflies and mosquitoes
in and out
the double lariat
song of the white throat,
pouring up moss-
pocked rock
into the high culture
of blueberries.

Inevitability

Outside the house
the light is laid
in bricks across the grass.

Damselflies,
farfetched as the rest of it,
warm their wings.

Depths of leaves
sunstruck at various depths,
of the day,

fading now
and then drawn
by the reach
of heedless shadows

which, as the light grows old,
grow outlandish
pulling the day back down
to black and restful rubble
where damselflies sleep brickwinged
where we hang our heads
fold our arms
around wind stilts

outcrops in darkness and sound
with skin to fill
handfuls of loamy night
to empty into the next implausible light.

Nightgale

The gull broken as only

a closely made thing can be

drags a crippled wing

like a sodden suitcase

away from a man handling a huge kite

over a bikini girl

tips its head at whirling shades

sheen of sea and sky

its alphabet and origin

form in flux

from artisan of flight and light

to beach rubbish

tucks into the nest

of the night's racked babel

of pure possibility

turned articulate breeze

murmuring non-repentance

As Only the Dead

Think of the language of Earth
as tactile memes
for every pulse
from acorn to bulldozer.

How it can't hear
us die through cities
because, apart
from the occasional attack
incurred while mowing or golfing,
who dies to ground anymore?

And how it hears at night
when the dog comes back from dark
with a beeping baby rabbit,
his instincts so strange to him
he can't think what to make
of the thing that belongs in his mouth,
he drops it in the grass.

Fairytale

They were sometimes separated
by their separate failings;
apart from the general wilt and crumble
twined in vacant transactions
overseen by chopped smiles,
the towering, weeping weight of what
had been unthought.

But long before the happy families
discharged therefrom had cleared,
revealing snapped roots, dry clods
like arms and clots,
they loved each other
for what each other loved,
kept house at the tower's foot,
the voices within thin and shrill.

She

She slit her eyes
broke open a poem
laid her finger on a word.

She cut it out,
framed and hung it.

She took it room to room,
a bare nail in each.

There had never been anything
like the breath of the word
at the head of her narrow bed.

Whenever anyone said it
she was bound tighter,
flowering according
to the system of law
issuing therefrom.

Her friends took note
cut up their books
framed words,
short words people had to use,
drove nails
into sheetrock and paneling
carted them anxiously
up and down stairs
in such numbers
they had no choice
but to be heard
in their dreams.

When they re-formed
in ways never before recorded—
there had never been such access to excess—
they burned their cuttings
called her a witch
and vowed
to never say her word.
This, too, organized her beauty

Waiting

elbow in elbow
pushing twin strollers
with your dozens
of different expensive purses
explosive prayers
shoes
don't get me started on tattoos
I can't see
black abaya floating through
the revolving door
shopping bags
bugs in scrubs and suits
and diers hunched and shuffling
canes   walkers
language and luggage on wheels
U.S.   Minnesota and Mayo flags
high rolling
the way you all swing your arms
or don't especially
if you're holding a paper cup
or a phone
or flowers
and there's one without

one foot past the other
into the future
where it all might happen
only the watcher is present
where it does
thinking nicely
that what you are thinking
can never be as important to you
as my sitting here
looking at it
through the window
of the Kahler Motel might be
to where we are both together going

Lydia

She has carefully washed her face and dressed for the day.
She is attentive while I check her arithmetic for neatly labeled
solutions, probably telling her to show her work because that's
what I say to everyone. She has a large python that she
brought to school once. She stands up straight at the corner
of my desk cleared off for her work. The rest is covered with
stories read and unread, worksheets, notes from parents
chameleoned in unopened mail from school supply companies.
Even this mess would have to grow to dimensions attributable
solely to mental illness before I'd be able to hide inside
from the danger of doing. Or I would have to shrink. There is a
good chance I was thinking about dreaming beneath the shell
of the dirty spoon when she took my glasses. I paused while
she cleaned them with a tissue and the stillness swelled,
cracking a brittle fastness, until twin pools of polished air fell
like geese on my eyes.

Tinnitis

I suppose this devilish breedle
rising through my feet,
into the lake of my body,
held within its shores of flesh,
washing around it organ islands,
screaming through the narrows of my neck,
churning the pond of my head,
could be an elemental lament,
punishment for thinking
I wouldn't mind deafness,
so seeming much
of sound, byproduct.

Like a Twilight Zone episode
where the character
is granted a carelessly stipulated wish,
I never imagined it would make me deaf
to its absence.

"That's Funny"

will hold, for life in general,
the way an appended amen suspends
a second thought,
but won't explain
how it moves in oceans

oceans, since nothing is seen
to enclose them,
defined by the things fallen
into them
and how they sink,
no place but down
to bear themselves
and whatever they hold in their teeth

how, exactly,
we breathe ourselves into our sins
until we float.

Sunday at the Farm

I forget how old I was
when I saw my grandpa's rifle
leaning in a corner of the entryway,
sat down on a stool, settled my head on the end.

But I remember well
the excitement of the void,
the wormhole, the All;
still, waiting, my own,
the kiss of my thumb and the pointer- polished trigger,
the gentle pressure,
anticipating the triumphant click,
another secret to keep
when, for no reason—
I recall well the missing reason—
I turned it around, wormholed the icebox,
and they came running
from the dining room.

Later, decades, someone said the blood drained from my face,
but I don't think it did.

Mere Choice

The wrong path looked fine
so I chose it and found
that it stopped
at a broken mill.

It was an optimistic choice
presuming a measure of life in the cards,

more steps
ending at endless dead-ends,
one of the beauties
and mercies of life:
the potential to annihilate by mere choice
all infinitudes
in favor of all others,
to sit down on the warm ruins
and study the reflective face of the river,
becoming and becoming again
and again.

Alumni Bulletin

Here you are
three years before vandals
pitched your darkness
from its cave,
silk shirt
straight, shiny hair,
Wonder Bread teeth

in an empty mouth
of dead grass,
empty threat
threaded into unfed branches,
pink mouth
set to swallow
the world
one word
at a time.

Now,
quaintly
patient
for what
to say
in narrowing time,
fresh days
squeezed around
wet weight
of accrued neglect.

Owled

Clean dishes and bedding
for what

I've hidden

where I find myself,
a cat in the woodpile,

there the handhold required
        your one tearless eye
to claim victory

in the absence of a stream
to bear away the drainage

Numbly humming
Nina Simone

the sun

the woolen drawl
from something
you've long
been tempted
to cross the center line
into

                you can't see the stars anymore
                not even here
                you should write a poem about that

Dog Box

I breathe the day's last lie,
come sweating to bed,
inebriated
by something that comes
from changing back
into something
clean and fitting,
the unimportant way I'm known
that gives me room
to wake up on the cold spot
where the dog leaked
in her sleep.

Room to crawl inside her box
let it attach the welcoming scent
the funky dog softness
let it turn my sickness three circles
curl me into a crescent
an open door
an Ellis Island if you like
for any dream
but mostly the ones from which I wake
with room to feel the fading grip
of coming back to life

Riptide, Valentine's Day

The last piece put you
on the wrong end
of an Impala,
us at the wrong end
of a minister.

But that's another puzzle.

A perfectly godless story
you might say:

the painstaking descent
through inebriate orbits
of bits of a smashed sister planet
in a tangled strand
of a dark second
spilled inside the lids
of our eyes.

Then the platitude blown
with nothing to do
but cut along
its dreamy passage
through lungs and heart
to hold them, somehow,
from breaching the bones:

"You may not feel him, but he's here."
"What?" says our deaf mother.
"What! sitting up
to the straw between my ribs,

driven up
a razored throat of ocean
through a ceiling of salt
to the heaving beach
aproned to an oceanfront
Fortress of Solitude
inert at the skirt of eternity
every action and inaction
a puzzle and piece composed of diminishing

puzzles and pieces
fueled by the futility

of the puzzle and piece
of the pathological puzzler himself,
of whom I observe
with an anguished rise
and fall and rise of ribs,
and in opposition
to the grave's frozen roses,
"So what."

Fetish

The foot
nicely hung
from its slung leg,
imperial heel, toes teasing hardwood,
inward arc of instep swelling
to outward arc of heel
and the bunion
forming the bottom
of the hourglass of the great toe,
pale and smooth
as mother-of-pearl,
dangling in fact
but, in effect, sculpture.

Castaway

One palm on my freckled forehead
the other on the dog
whose contentment I trust.

Now and then he moves his head
adjusts a leg
runs his tongue wetly
along the roof of his mouth
so I know he's made himself
again as comfortable

as the sleepy socks drooping from their drawer
as the bird droppings, very badge of contentment
on the arms of the chair we share
in a landscape of clothing, books, bags.

We could be flotsam
flung from the sea.

There! Looking out
from a lobster
or a shoe
my favorite pen!
Mightier than a horde
of Dutch boys' fingers
stuck into the holes
sunk into the day
by thoughts of its lostness.

If I died now—this again—
the EMTs might say "he was ready,"
when clearly I'm not
or maybe I'm wrong,
all this nothing done.

Shifting my gaze out the window
I think I'd rather
let the assortment of greens
through the leaves of the oak tree
grow wilder for another weekend

if it weren't for the neighbors
and their windows.

Besides, the cat would like to be excused.
I set my foot on the floor.
The small dog
of the buckled gums
and bad manners
cracks an eye.

wondering

if the boxes and shoes
and litter of papers on the floor
are metaphor or reflection
of an idle mind
reclining in its skull

if the milk in my bowl
is metaphor
for the circular light
it reflects

when the kitten jumps into my lap
a purring furnace
morphing me
into the guy who's late for work again.

Still

Without the thrashing snake
it is till:
a cross, i,
a pair of trainless rails
a vacant trail
an empty aisle
an empty i'll.

Still, till
does not become
still till
after the thrashing snake.

Detaching the snake and cross
leaves those of Christian tilt
mortally ill.

Northern Religion

God is merely the angle,
merely the nook
you would have to be an angel to see

and I'm more nearly
a howling bear,
lean-eyed, hidden
like prayer in fragile light,
denied a den of chalky feathers,
a pair of pretty arms,

because I won't talk
about my day
with my mouth full
of moonlight.

Open River

The way thumb and index
extend pen to paper
weighing the nib
exposes my skin,
written in sunlight and stitches.

Cradled in muscle and vein,
slanted across a tapering void,
conspiring the breakup
of winter ice.

The greasy middle
the grainy edge
of what moves
into and out
of my fingertips,
each the end of its own soft curve
touching back.

Shared Space

You met Orion at the door
his composure, as always, intact.
Sat awhile, then brought me, caught deep
in a dream of trees
one wholesome fact:
Rigel and Betelgeuse
the brightest of the fold
and without distraction went to sleep
your chair pushed up to the threshold
window slid to showcase
the leaves eating the light
that wears them for breakfast,
a marriage made in space.

Natural Causes

In dusty houses
with sallow shades
floating ghostly
past books, pictures
broken furniture
unconnected
disengaged
functional rubble
of teeth, knees, hips
skipping the charters to Branson,
afternoon performances
of Hamlet

writing in their journals
how the view from the end of the road
mirrors the view from the beginning:
a thoughtless line
vining to mind,
a heart of treetops,
vanishing unsurprised
through the floorboards.

Photograph From My Mother's House

3 stretched M's for birds
the sky washed
blushing and blue

a girl, a curtain
a gray gravel road
in early summer

illegible presence
curious blur
trusting ghost
of your dying

who believes in the living
you see through the frame
what the evident-when-developed
photo-bomber will jellyfish out of
90 years hence

into the back of a shiny black car
sky an unwashed white
i-less dot
   we listened while you slept
in the back
of a mind
rolling slowly
   with what you kept of the world
to keep from slipping
on the white road
of powdered bone

negative of a clear December night
bucking off the windows

Affair

Playdate planned,
you drank a glass of filtered water,
"dead" they call it
because of a chemical imbalance,
raised a smile
to the woman who gave you sons
now grown and gone.
The yellow lab got all the strokes,
an honest evasion,
sufficient provision against suspicion.

Did you feel a tingle, unlocking
The SUV waiting in the driveway

                    did you buckle up?

to bear you to the shooting range

                    signal lane changes?
                    take note of the caution
                    on the side-view mirror?
                    pause after you took your
                    foot off the brake
                    to feel yourself breathing?
                    its mathematics?
                    its perfection?

before you stepped out of the vehicle
but not the parking lot?

Breathing

Extreme ahead of his time,
the old naturalist climbs a far-flung fir
flexing like a runner's lung,
the howl and spike ripping clouds
to busty shreds mid-gallop,
slapped hard alive
by the squall's studded paw

and deaf to the winter
wren working
its lungs in the roots
of a fallen poplar,
dispatching into
the storm an unpunishable
trill and chant
apart from the raging
insignificance
of the moment,
apart from the mercenary germ
burning it back
to dirt and trees.

Gyotaku

We needed another fish, so one, a pretty
pumpkinseed, was scooped from the aquarium
and left in an empty sink until it stopped
flopping and gulping. Taken up, wiped dry
brushed with ink, pressed onto a white t-shirt
rinsed off, passed around, scales, tail,
gills, all around the eye, inked
over a different color, sometimes a florid
combination: orange ventral, green
dorsal, a yellow crescent over the gills,
covered with a paper towel,
pressed hard every inch
for a detailed print minus the eye,
indicated by a vacant circle
as if eaten out by a scavenger.
When it was over, someone, in casual
hope or slender regret, dropped it back
into the tank where it filled itself with air,
woke, and swam, indistinguishable
from the other fish until it died.

Goose

I bought him a hamburger
and had him euthanized
he didn't like the first needle
in his leg
lifted his head
knew enough
to buck and whine

to the one who took you
from eight days wasting
in a cage you apologized
he said it's ok
before you could believe it or not
the bomb to your heart went off

Hawk

Patience spilled
from a ghost hole

Feathers edge-up
now folded and gone
from the tsunami of my sight

behind leprous leaves
rotting stoppers
sunk into the sky

poised to break over
the freshly cut grass
and my father's body

Bench

I loaded into the truck
from the end of a driveway
because it was free

set it in the yard,
a seat for the sun

for the leaves'
sharp shadows

the hidden whip
of the cardinal

the parasitic silence
inside the trees

and, from the brush pile,
the rasp of the wren
spending its penny lungs

the Delphic lichen
rivaling the spaces
between the leaves
in its shades
from gray to green:

marks that things made
will degrade
into meaning,
hearable

as when my dying
wakes early
to talk a little.
And because it's not talking to me
and I get to forget each word
I listen and hear my part,
expendable element
whose absence claps
into a fresh perfection.

Fox

On nights when I fail
to grow soft paws for sleeping
I drop my bones
in a gully and wait—
the rhythmic snap of her approach—
to be bowed one piece at a time
over the path and touched
to the crescent tips of the careless tongues
        of her hungry young,
held in the new light
of their teeth, and given down
to the warm, dark dens of their bellies
till morning
springs rabbits
from the brush
of my tail.

Sleep Song

Her abrupt heft,
plump on the quilt,
(but deft in the dark)
under which
we expect to embark
upon sleep
beats all
like a heavy heart
an essential part
escaped the skin,
spent and purring
beneath my chin.

Cat at 4 A.M.

Self-swallowing sky in mute
black flower, swimmers bracing
to break the trembling waves
a brace and hover
in the perfect pause
of placed charges,
suspended in a caught end breath

    skyless fliers
    skyless rain

a flash of scorched orchids
in beds of broken glass,
the glazed eye of a sharded horse,

a final evasion:
hoarse crunch of boots on glass,
breath released,
oceans collapse,
I fly into orbit
on the cold, hard, moon of her nose.

Town Birds

Clamor behind the green
restaurant dumpster
aflutter and flagrant
in their gray aprons
and warm plume
of fries, cigarettes,
and grilled buns.
They flock on the steps
heads on quick swivels
amid the not disagreeable flies,
light price for the luxury
of loud laughter

and the mute passerby
skimming the waves
over the sidewalk
en route
to a clean library bay
where she bends
hidden, unharried
her long neck,
poised over suspended words,
bare feet sunk
in the cold carpet.

The Bird Outside the Library

I'd like to see a ballerina
with all her muscle control
lie so serenely splashed
as this bird corpse
this motorcycle wreck
rained from the sky
down a metal pipe
into the street,
the kind of thing you might sit on a porch
and drink your tea away for a month
while it evaporates
back up through the leaves.

Ok, Thirty Minutes Then

At last I'm ready to dispose
of this snarling body
of staring details
which, till now, have been coddled into line.
Then I'll be able to enjoy the cat

who's just jumped
onto the back of the chair
and draped himself
across my neck
like one of those hideous stoles
mostly old ladies
used to wear to church,
glass eyes and bared teeth
looking for a phantom foot to chew off,
in Dantesque distress
for the coming
of merciful moths.   Except

the cat is heaving his belly
on the back of my neck,
pushing his slitted eyes
and wet mouth behind my ear,
purring furiously,
not at all like a detail.

Breaking the Picture Plane

When the rain stops, the leaves, though suspended on their stems,
are as still as Durer's hare, his piece of turf,
revealed, only by the occasional drip from
a leaf above causing one to bounce on its
stem, to exist in this dimension.

Catbird, cardinal, chickadee, crow, silent
as the drinking earth, the fresh light; as the
leaves are still.

Was a time I'd have left the house for the
trees, in a state of mild panic at missing
whatever would happen next and how. And
there was a dog named Jack who was
eventually struck by a car near the
cemetery, and had his hip fixed with screws.

Now I read poetry and look at the window
for who I am until the puppy, fat as a monk,
sets to barking back the world.

Cave Hills

Here, where you came
to quench your affliction
--there were many—
for taloned birds,
we were eels
in runnels
of slicked down sunlight
sliding past hoary pine
and prickly pear,
sparks of laughter
arcing the unwilling
lawn chair,
shade,
eddy,
you,
brooding the ocean.

Feather

In the perfect middle of nowhere
insects sing in the middle distance.
I'm in the shade.
The birds across the ravine are in the sun.
Later, it will be hot.

I pick things up. Broken bits.
Put them on a rock
where they seem okay.

I watch the birds.
They don't mind being seen
but they don't sit still for it either.

Something flutters close by
but I hold still.
If I stay long enough
like this
I'll see something marvelous I suppose,
something that will kill me,
make it harder to earn a living.

I'd like to see a cougar
but I don't have to.

The sky is gray and puffy like rocks.

I've got a good spot on the edge
next to a yellow flower.

There may be ghosts
but I don't believe there's an afterlife to speak of
unless I'm looking at it.

Dropped off a cliff
would be a good afterlife
if you could get it;
a way to be sure
that what you don't understand
still makes sense,
to say that endlessly.

I move with the shade

wishing for a long tail
to brush away late waking flies
when a long primary feather
falls out of the sky
from where I climb down
to shake it from a branch
to pick it up.

Last September

It wasn't the sun-pinked trunks
of the pine trees
or my still stride,
outside-in as
the glade's golden white
through a hollow trunk.
This is no impression. It happened
as surely as the leaves turned the colors of spring
warblers, earth-tilted
into sudden contentment:
the purred question
of the barred owl
hung motionless
mustered nothing
from the deep seeing crows
who dropped their bodies
out of darkness,
supplanted danger with light
as in pictures that,
from time to time, include us.

A Family Reunion

"If we're lucky,
until we walk around the block,
look out the window,
see
the last heart breakingly
beguiling thing
 we are capable of seeing:
the new to the world squirrel,
four feet trampolining off the earth,
running the rise
to the base of a great tree,
rolling down. Twice.
Or two crows billing,
on a power line
carved into the sunrise,"
I answer unhelpfully and 5 years late
to my mother's question:
How long must we live?

Again. Until our lives shrink so tightly
around our memories
they burst out
and disintegrate like old manuscripts:
out of inertia,
into the bright heat
at the splice of erasure and untakeable happiness where,
our blessings having returned themselves,
we arrive.

Recompense

As we shared
our disappointment
in the movie

a deer appeared
in the headlights.

Not the hypnotized idiom,
but fully functional,

unable to imagine
the way things die,

not transfixed
the way I was

by the stilled, strobed
deer-shaped cavity,

how its gravity
crushed the day,

eyeing life
on the other side

Good Friday

But I'm still the same brute
who sinned in his sleep last night,
who decades ago
stuck alone with God,
left town

for a row of red deities
in Red Rover formation,
old bottles of perfume
and liquor on a canyon wall.

It was exciting,
the best I recall
before the fog slipped in
all fuzzy feet and Cheshire grin.

Now here's an old dog
tired from his morning excursion.
The pictures on the wall are framed.
I can move them where I please.
They don't look back.

I wonder what we'd be doing
in the desert today
comes back the reflection
something had to happen

that's how the dinosaurs
and Bible got here.

I don't know anything about absolution.
That's Something's job.
Call it Carrie Fisher.

I know a little bit about second thoughts.
It's better to be someone else's.

Black Hole

It escapes with a crunch
our home-bound headlights
into the out-bound.

Is it the same deer
that swallowed the day a year ago
in this very same spot?

Frenetic squad car lights
frisk every fold of April 8
whose whetted night
discloses no doubt
of death's intelligence

in the sprawled body,
skin split neatly
along the backbone
the way winter and spring
fall apart at the equator,

or whether the corpse
collapsed or exploded into being,
its seasons emerging
into the pool of light spilled
from a gently bent SUV,
into the earth
from which they leapt
an eternal moment ago.

No doubt in the thud of a period
suggesting an unseen sentence.

Planting

The leaves of the birthday oak,
finally and finely tanned,
crowd toward the garage
where, in older age,
I'll watch the squirrels
from this window and chair,
envy, between chapters, naps,
and trips to the john,
their careless collection
of acorns dropped
on the black beach of its roof.

This year made a single green acorn,
the first,
whose pleasure's been squirreled
in a furrow, poised to sprout,
as some say
certain images from life may do
at the moment of our dying.

World Made Innuendo

A little snow
a little gray
don't hurt
the way snowdrop, bloodroot, Siberian squill,
open for business,
grackles working on their nests,
on the tomes of their brief lives,
the Pollacked egg swirling down the drain
of the left nest, rescued
into a rodent's mouth,
hurt:
suggestions of the unslowable insoluble.

So yeah,
I like a little snow
speaking only of itself.

It's the greens and flowers disembarking,
the endless writing of names
making of sense
in the river's ripples and glints,
the friendly exchange of space
between leaves and air,
the steady demolition of the lock that worked
by not existing,
that secured
it all from
mute ruin
that advises us to despise
the horizon.

Craig Evenson is a public school teacher for 37 years. Now he's an old English major camping in the fall and spring. He lives in Northfield, Minnesota with his wife, Margaret, two dogs, two parrots, and a cat. This is his first collection of poems.

www.ingramcontent.com/pod-product-compliance
Lightning Source LLC
Chambersburg PA
CBHW011231120626
46549CB00008B/3232